{{code creator}}

CODING ACTIVITIES FOR
CODING ROBOTS WITH LEGO MINDSTORMS®

Emilee Hillman

ROSEN PUBLISHING

Published in 2022 by The Rosen Publishing Group, Inc.
29 East 21st Street, New York, NY 10010

Copyright © 2022 by The Rosen Publishing Group, Inc.

First Edition

Library of Congress Cataloging-in-Publication Data

Names: Hillman, Emilee, author.
Title: Coding activities for coding robots with LEGO Mindstorms® / Emilee Hillman.
Description: First edition. | New York : Rosen Publishing, 2022. | Series: Code creator | Includes bibliographical references and index.
Identifiers: LCCN 2019015774| ISBN 9781725341081 (library bound) | ISBN 9781725341074 (pbk.)
Subjects: LCSH: Robots—Programming—Juvenile literature. | Robots—Models—Juvenile literature. | LEGO Mindstorms toys.
Classification: LCC TJ211.2 .H476 2022 | DDC 629.8/925269—dc23
LC record available at https://lccn.loc.gov/2019015774

Manufactured in the United States of America

Some of the images in this book illustrate individuals who are models. The depictions do not imply actual situations or events.

CPSIA Compliance Information: Batch #CSRYA22. For further information contact Rosen Publishing, New York, New York at 1-800-237-9932.

Find us on

Contents

Introduction

At their most basic, robots are machines that move based on instructions that are given by humans. How are these instructions transmitted from a human brain to a robot's parts? The answer is no surprise: computer programming. There are a variety of different types of programming languages that can be used to program different types of robots, and robotic technology is becoming more and more

Robotic arms, such as this, are among the most basic—and most useful—kinds of automation. Even moving this single limb requires a lot of coding.

commonplace. There are robots of many varieties being manufactured for all ages and purposes. Many robots are being created specifically to teach students to program, preparing them for computer programming at a more advanced level. One of these robots is the LEGO Mindstorms® EV3 robotics core kit made by LEGO Education.

LEGO Mindstorms® EV3 robotics kits include a variety of building bricks, a programming brick, motors, and sensors—and these components can be used to create a wide range of robots. The LEGO

The LEGO Mindstorms® EV3 robotics kits allow you to imagine and create your own robots and customize their movements through programming.

Mindstorms® EV3 application is used to program the robot using LEGO's custom-built version of a block programming language. This application is available for Android, iOS, Windows, and macOS. However, the more robust features of the software are only available on the Windows and macOS operating systems.

The LEGO Mindstorms® EV3 robotics kit comes with instructions for building a basic driving base and directions for slight modifications to add each of the sensors to the driving base, as well as the medium motor to add an arm to the base. The hardware, of course, is just one part of the puzzle, however. The other necessary component is the software application. Instructions for downloading and accessing this software can be found at: https://www .lego.com/en-us/mindstorms/downloads.

After using the LEGO Mindstorms® EV3 robotics kits to build a physical robot, the next step is to program that robot using the appropriate software. The version of the application necessary for programming will depend on the number of blocks used to build the robot.

Start the coding process by adding a new program, making sure to give it an appropriate name— MyFirstRobot, for example. The workspace that opens will take up most of the screen and will always have a Start block in the center. Along the bottom of the screen, there are different tabs; each tab contains a specific category of programming blocks. These

Take the time to familiarize yourself with the parts in your kit. There are countless different kinds of bricks and additional modifications that could be used to change your robot.

activities will make use of these various blocks in different ways, and they can be completed using any version of LEGO's programming application.

Mindstorms® EV3 robots are able to download programming through a wired or Bluetooth connection. It is also possible to do limited programming directly through the brick.

With a robot built and the program constructed, the next step is generally to test the program and the robot together, to make sure they are both working properly. There are two different ways to connect a device to a robot to transfer the program. If it was coded using a computer, it can be transferred by connecting a USB connector cord (which should be included in any LEGO Mindstorms® EV3 kit) from the computer to the robot and then downloading the program and telling it to run. This is why it is very important to name the program something recognizable, so that you know which program to

A mobile application makes it very easy to program your Mindstorms® EV3 robot via a Bluetooth connection.

run when selecting it on the robot. If the program was coded using a mobile device, the robot can be connected to that mobile device through the use of Bluetooth. After connecting the robot and mobile device together, download and run the appropriate program to test it out.

LEGO Mindstorms® EV3 robots can be turned on by pressing the button in the center of the main control brick. To turn off the robot, press the gray button directly under the edge of the display screen until asked whether the robot should be powered down. Then, use the quad buttons to toggle to the check and the center button to select the check.

It is possible to name the robot, and this can be done right on the brick itself. In fact, it is also possible to do some limited programming directly through the brick without the need for another device. To name the robot, use the right-side button on the selection of buttons on the front of the brick to scroll over to the settings menu (represented by a wrench image). Then, use the bottom button of the quad to toggle down to Brick Name; use the center button to select that option. Use the buttons to toggle and select each letter in the desired name and then click on the check mark to finally change the name.

Activity 1

Get Moving

This activity will show off two different code blocks—steering and tank—that will get the robot's motors moving. Each of these blocks will need to be altered by changing the modes, parameters, and values associated with them. See how each of these will change the robot's movements to move forward. Which block is most effective for moving straight ahead?

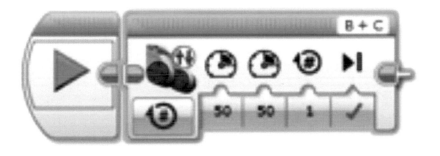

Move Tank block example

Make sure the robot is fully charged before starting a new activity. It is also important to make sure the robot is turned on and connected to whatever device is being used to program it, whether that is through Bluetooth or the USB connector cord.

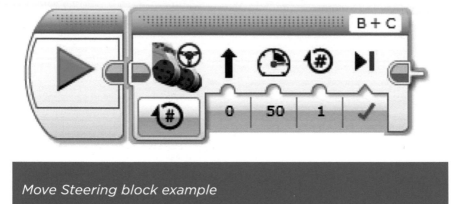

Move Steering block example

Start off by opening the LEGO Mindstorms® EV3 coding application on any supported device. Launch a new program in the application and name it Get Moving. Check to see that the large motors are connected through the B and C ports in the bottom right-hand corner of the application; take note of the angle value for both motors. On the bottom of the screen, there is a green tab that can be used to access action blocks. There are three action blocks that can be used to control the large motors: Large Motor block, Move Steering block, and Move Tank block. This activity will focus on the latter two.

Drag the Move Steering block into the workspace and attach it to the Start block that should already be in place. Notice that the Move Steering block has a small image of the two large motors with a steering wheel to help identify the purpose of this block. Below this image is where the mode of the steering block can be modified. The default mode when adding this code block to a program is set for

On for rotations, which is shown as a number symbol with a circle around it. It could also be set for On for seconds or On for degrees, so choose any of these modes. Once selected, it is also necessary to change the parameters. There are two changes to make with a steering block: steering (determining the heading or direction of the robot) and power (determining the speed of the robot). Finally, update the value based on the mode chosen. It will be necessary to change either the number of rotations the motors make, the number of seconds the motors will run, or the number of degrees the motors will rotate—each according to the mode selected.

Click the Start block on the program to execute it and see how it runs. Take note of how far the robot was able to move based on the parameters and values entered into the program.

Now, remove the Move Steering block from the program and add in the Move Tank block. Notice that the Move Tank block has a small image for the two large motors with a track symbol to help identify the purpose of this block. As with the Move Steering block, play around with the mode, parameters, and value of the block. Notice that with the Move Steering block, the power parameter for each motor can be modified separately. What would happen if you chose two different power values? Click the Start block to execute the program and see how it runs.

With this experience in mind, which block is easier to use? Which is more efficient for moving straight ahead?

Activity 2

Maze Master

There is a lot more to robots than just making them move forward. The first step to this activity is using masking tape or electrical tape to outline a maze for the robot to navigate through. Find a space on the floor to make the maze; it can take any shape and be as simple or complex as you like. This will be the course through which the robot will run based on its programming.

Clever use of the Move Tank block will be necessary to make it through the maze. Mastering the measurement of straight and angled lengths and distances and adjusting parameters and values will help make the navigation successful. You will need to be precise and persistent—a program like this one will require several iterations before it is done just right.

Open the LEGO Mindstorms® EV3 application on the device of your choice. Start a new program in the application and name it Maze Master. Make sure that the large motors are connected through the B and C ports in the bottom right-hand corner of the application; take note of the angle value for both motors.

Before starting up the program, make a plan based on the maze—write down the steps that the robot will have to take to go through the maze. For example:

1. Move forward about 12 inches.
2. Make a right-hand turn.
3. Move forward about 8 inches.
4. Make a slight left turn.

Once you have a basic plan in place, then you can start creating the program. Try to follow the steps you just outlined to guide the robot through the maze.

As a note: it is important to make sure that the robot starts in the exact same place and position for each iteration of the program. After adding each step to the program, it will be helpful to test the program and reflect on its effectiveness before making more additions. When making changes to the program, it is very important that only one parameter or value is changed at a time. For instance, when the robot needs to make a turn but it has not turned far enough to continue to the next part of the maze, first try to change just the steering parameter of the robot to increase the angle at which it is turning. If that is not enough, try adjusting just the number of rotations instead of the steering value. Do not try to change both parameters at once—that is likely to cause more problems than it solves.

On the bottom of the programming screen, open the green tab that contains action blocks. Drag the Move Steering block into the workspace and attach it to the Start block. Each step of the maze will require a new block—perhaps even more than one block for certain turns, depending on the complexity of the maze. After adding each block to the program and testing it, make notes on the original planning sheet about the block used for each step and the parameters and values needed to complete that step of the program.

The end of the activity comes once you have created a successful program to run through the entire maze—start to finish—using a single program. It will likely take quite a while to get to this point, but once the Maze Master program is complete, it can be reused to navigate through the maze forever.

Activity 3

Shape It Up

One important step in robot mastery is learning to use the loop block to program a robot more efficiently. The goal? Create shapes with the least number of blocks possible. This activity will require a basic knowledge of geometry: how many sides do certain shapes have and what type of angles are used to create different shapes?

Start off by opening the LEGO Mindstorms® EV3 application, starting a new program in the application, and naming it Shape It Up. Make sure that the large motors are connected through the B and C ports in the bottom right-hand corner of the application; take note of the angle value for both motors.

Since this activity is all about shapes, start off with something simple: a square. On a piece of paper, draw a basic square. After drawing the shape, think about the steps required to create it. Write these steps down, and be very specific. For example:

1. Draw a straight line that is 2 inches long.
2. Turn ninety degrees to the right.
3. Draw a straight line that is 2 inches long.
4. Turn ninety degrees to the right.
5. Draw a straight line that is 2 inches long.
6. Turn ninety degrees to the right.
7. Draw a straight line that is 2 inches long.

Robots—and all computer programs—need very explicit directions to run a program, even one as simple as moving in a shape pattern. One block of code is needed for running in a straight line, another block of code is needed for turning the robot so that it is in position to create the next line, etc. These steps are repeated over and over for the number of sides needed to make a target shape: in this case, four times.

On the bottom of the application's screen, open up the orange tab to use flow control blocks. Drag the Loop block into the workspace and attach it to the Start block. A Loop block allows you to repeat the blocks of code that are housed within that loop for a specific number of times, until something else happens, or even infinitely. To use the loop block, place other blocks of code within the loop and then choose the conditional setting that is required to accomplish the task at hand—in this case, repeating directions a set number of times to draw a shape. Within the Loop block, there will need to be a Move Steering block that is set to move forward for a specific value. There will also need to be a Move Tank block, set to turn at a ninety-degree angle (adjust values until finding the right ones to create a ninety-degree turn). Then, click on the infinity symbol on the Loop block and change the conditional from unlimited to the number value that reflects how many times the looped code should repeat itself. Set this to Count, which looks like a number symbol (#), and then set the value to 4.

Click the Start button to execute the program and determine its success. How well did it draw out a square shape?

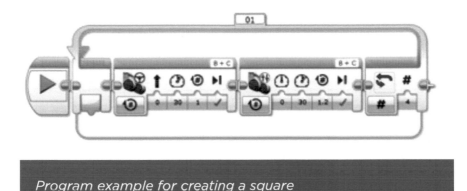

Program example for creating a square

Try repeating these steps to draw a shape with a different number of sides. Remember: a shape can only ever contain 360 degrees. That means it is necessary to calculate both the number of sides and the angles of each turn when looking at other shapes. For example, a hexagon has six sides, so the Loop block will need to repeat six times—but the angle also needs to be adjusted from ninety degrees to sixty degrees. Here is a tip for calculating angles: divide 360 (the number of degrees in a shape) by the number of sides (i.e., 4 for a square, 6 for a hexagon) to figure out what angles the robot should take.

Activity 4

Stop Right There!

One great thing about robots is that they are machines that are capable of more than just moving forward or turning. There are many attachments and accessories that can be added to a robotic machine to make it do some incredible things—one example is the LEGO Mindstorms® EV3 color sensor. In this activity, the color sensor will be used to program a loop, and the color sensor conditional statement will have the

Example of a robot with an attached color sensor

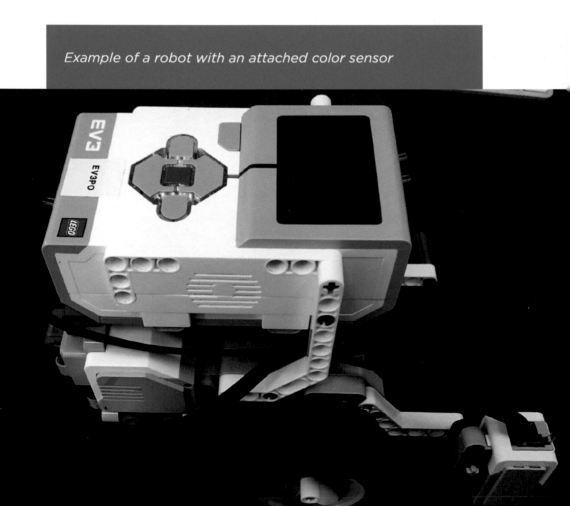

robot move forward until it reaches a line drawn in a specific color that tells it to stop.

Since this activity makes use of the color sensor, make sure to attach it to the front of the robot. It should be facing down. The color sensor can both detect color and measure light intensity.

Once the sensor is attached, open the LEGO Mindstorms® EV3 application and start up a new program. It should be named Stop Right There. Make sure that the large motors are connected through the B and C ports in the bottom right-hand corner of the application; take note of the angle value for both motors. In the same location, the color sensor should also display as being detected in port three.

On the bottom of the application, open the orange tab to use the flow control blocks. Drag the Loop block into the workspace and attach it to the Start block. The Loop block can be used for more than just repeating something a set number of times; it also permits the use of other conditional statements. In this case, the robot should move forward until it reaches a colored line. That makes the detection and identification of a color the necessary conditional for this program. Before programming any further, find a marker or pen that is black, blue, green, yellow, red, or white. Make sure the color is a good contrast to whatever surface the robot is moving across. With a coloring utensil in hand, draw a thick line on a sheet of paper and place it a short distance away from the robot's starting point. This will be the location at which the robot should stop.

In the application, click back to the green tab and add a Move Steering block inside of the Loop block. Set the Move Steering block to On mode so that the motor remains running until the robot detects a colored line. Consider adjusting the speed value of the block as well. If the robot is moving too quickly, the sensor may not be able to detect a colored line before it completely passes over the line without triggering the conditional.

Next, set the conditional for the Loop block. Click on the infinity symbol and hover over the Color Sensor option and select Color. Change the value of the color to match the line that represents the stopping point of the robot. Before settling on a color to use for the program, it may be helpful to test the sensor's detection of different colors. To do this, hold the sensor up to a color sample and see what value is being read by looking at the bottom-right corner of the screen.

Click the Start button to execute the program and see if it worked. Was the robot able to move forward, detect the colored line, and stop accordingly? Make adjustments to the speed of the motors in the Move Steering block if the robot sped right over the line without detecting it. If that does not work, it may be necessary to change the color of the stop line to something that will be easier for the color sensor to recognize.

Activity 5

Follow the Line

The color sensor attachment can be used for more than just sensing colors. In this activity, the robot will be programmed to follow a line based on the reflected light intensity that is detected by the color sensor. This will require the use of a new concept: the Switch block, which acts as an if-then variable to create a program that allows the robot to turn toward and away from the line to follow the edge of it. This will also require the Loop block so that the robot is continuously using the sensor to analyze light intensity to seek to move toward or away from the line.

Make sure the color sensor is still attached securely to the robot before beginning this activity. Then, start the LEGO Mindstorms® EV3 application and open a new program named Follow the Line. Make sure that the large motors are connected through the B and C ports in the bottom right-hand corner of the application; take note of the angle value for both motors. In the same location, the color sensor should also display as being detected in port three.

Open up the orange tab on the bottom of the screen to use the flow control blocks. Drag the Loop block into the workspace and attach it to the Start block. In this case, the robot should use the color sensor to continuously search for the line. That means the Loop block should stay on the unlimited conditional for this program. With that set, drag and place a Switch block inside of the Loop block.

The Switch block helps the robot make decisions, choosing one action if the variable is true and a different action if the variable is false. It acts as an if-then conditional, giving the robot two choices depending on the variables it can detect. If-then statements are extremely common in programming. Quite simply, they tell a program that if something is true, then it should take a specific action. If it is not true, something else should happen. This has countless uses in software applications, from the most basic to the most advanced.

The default variable for the Switch block here is for the touch sensor—this will need to be changed to be Color—Compare Reflected Light Intensity. Inside of the Switch block, there are two choices of code for the robot to run depending on the variable. If yes— represented by the check mark—the robot runs that string. If no, the robot runs the other string of code. Inside the check mark, drag a Move Tank block, set the mode to On and set B motor to speed 40 and C motor to speed 0. Inside the X mark, drag a Move Tank block, set the mode to On and set B motor to speed 0 and C motor to speed 40.

With all that set, it is time to make a line. Choose a color with which to make the line; make sure that the line color and the floor color are contrasting. Draw the line so that it zigs and zags, but it should

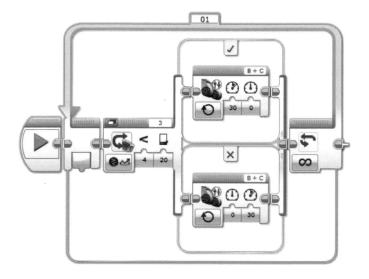

Example of a "follow the line" program

be continuous (with no breaks) and it should not contain any extreme angles. Test the light intensity readings of each (the line and the floor) by holding the robot's color sensor up to the colors and looking at the reading in the bottom-right corner for port three. Make sure the value used for the reflected light intensity is accurate: the line color should be higher than the value in the Switch block and the floor color should be lower than that value.

If the values detected by the color sensor do match up, there are two ways to fix the issue. The first way would be to pick a different color for the line—one that will measure as being above the Switch block's value. The second way is to manually adjust the value in the Switch block so that the intensity value for the line is above it, and the intensity value for the floor is below it. This method is probably easier.

With all that set, place the robot so that the color sensor looks down at the beginning of the line. Click the Start button to execute the program: Was the robot able to follow the line? How might the program be modified to make the robot follow the line more smoothly?

Make modifications to your program to see if it is possible to improve the performance of the robot. Try adjusting the speed of the motors or the value of the reflected light intensity in the Switch block. Did any of those changes help make the program run better? Why or why not?

Activity 6

Pump the Brakes

Another important tool for the LEGO Mindstorms®
EV3 robot is its ultrasonic sensor. Similar to the color
sensor attachment, the ultrasonic sensor can be
used to gather information about the world outside
the robot, which can then be used by a program
to make a decision. This activity will be based on
programming the robot to stop at an object using the
ultrasonic sensor. This will be done by testing different
parameters and values to see how close the robot
can get to a wall before stopping. Then, the program
will be modified to stop at the wall, then back up or
turn around.

   The first step in this activity is to attach the
ultrasonic sensor to the front of the robot. This sensor
can measure the distance between the robot and an
object using high-frequency sound waves. The next
step is to open the coding application and start up
a new program named Pump the Brakes. Make sure
that the large motors are connected through the B
and C ports in the bottom right-hand corner of the
application. In the same location, the ultrasonic sensor
should also display as being detected in port four.

   On the bottom of the programming screen, open
the orange tab to access the flow control blocks. Drag
the Loop block into the workspace and attach it to
the Start block. In this case, the Loop block should tell
the robot to use the ultrasonic sensor to continuously

Example of a driving base robot with ultrasonic sensor attached

send high-frequency sound waves out in front of it as a way of measuring its distance from other objects. The conditional of this Loop block should be changed from unlimited to the Ultrasonic—Compare Distance option. There is a suboption here to change the unit of measurement between inches and centimeters; either selection will work. Make sure the parameter is set to less than and the value set to 10. This means that the robot's motors will run until it reaches less than 10 units of measure (inches or centimeters) from a detected object. Switch to the action tab on the bottom of the workspace and drag a Move Steering block into the Loop block. Change the mode of the Move Steering block to On and reduce the speed to 30 or below.

With all that programmed in, find a wall and place the robot so that it is more than ten units of measure from that wall. Click the Start button to execute the program; was it able to detect the object in front of it and stop within ten units of measure? Use a measurement tool, like a ruler, to check the accuracy.

Next, try modifying the program so that the robot stops closer to the object in front of it. This is done by lowering the value in the Loop block to something less than 10. After that, try another modification. For instance, add another Move Steering block after the Loop block that will have the robot back up after reaching the chosen distance threshold for the ultrasonic sensor conditional.

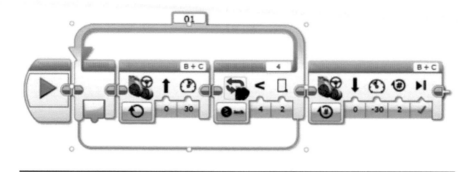

Example of the program with suggested modifications

After playing around with some values and parameters, how close was the robot able to get to the wall without touching it? How accurate was the sensor in stopping the robot at the programmed distance? For example: if the program told the robot to stop at 5 inches away from the wall, how close was it to 5 inches?

Touchy Touchy

There are many ways of programming a robot to begin executing its code. One way is to tell the robot to start moving when a touch sensor attachment is pressed. Aside from starting movement, it is also possible to modify the program to play a sound or change the display image when the touch sensor is pressed. These options will be the focus of this activity.

Example of a driving base robot with touch sensor attached

For this activity, it will be necessary to incorporate the touch sensor into the design of the robot—a good location will be on the top, so it can easily be accessed. The touch sensor is essentially a button that detects when it has been pressed or released.

Begin by starting a new program called Touchy Touchy in the LEGO Mindstorms® EV3 application. Make sure that the large motors are connected through the B and C ports in the bottom right-hand corner of the application. In the same location, the touch sensor should also display as being detected in port one.

Access the orange tab on the bottom of the screen and use the flow control blocks here. Drag the Wait block into the workspace and attach it to the Start block. The Wait block asks the robot to wait for a specific condition to be met before moving to the next step of the program. In this case, the robot needs to wait until its touch sensor has been pressed; then, it should move.

Change the mode of the Wait block to Touch Sensor—Compare—State. Make sure the parameter is set for 1, indicating that when the touch sensor is pressed, it will complete the Wait block and move to the next block. Next, click on the green tab to add an action block. Choose either Move Steering or Move Tank to add after the Wait block. Change the mode, parameters, and values to your own specifications.

Click the Start button to execute the program. Did the robot move as expected after the touch sensor was pressed? How could the code be modified to add different actions—aside from moving forward—when the touch sensor is pressed?

Try making changes to the program so that the robot completes a different action after the touch sensor is pressed. Maybe the robot should play a sound effect when the touch sensor is pressed. This could be coded by dragging the Move block off the Start block and off the screen. Then, replace that block with the Sound block and change the mode to Play File. On the top of the block—where the port for a sensor is typically displayed—the name of the sound file that will be played will be shown instead. By clicking on that name, it is possible to view all of the premade sound files and select a different sound file to try.

After that, try another modification. For instance, maybe the display block on the robot should display a new image or a message when the touch sensor has been pressed. Follow the same procedure used for the Sound block to add, set up, and change a Display block.

What other uses could you imagine for the touch sensor? If the touch sensor was moved somewhere else—not on the top of the robot—what functions could it have to make the robot more useful or intuitive?

Activity 8

Robot Arm

Up until now, these activities have been based around having the robot avoid interaction with other objects. However, robots can be used to accomplish simple tasks—such as moving an object—if they have the right attachment. In this activity, the robot will be programmed to move something using its medium motor and a lifting arm accessory.

To accomplish all this, it will be necessary to add the medium motor with an arm attached that will be controlled by that motor. The medium motor is smaller and lighter than the large motors and responds a little more quickly—but it is programmed in pretty much the same way as the large motors.

Once the motor and arm have been attached, open the LEGO Mindstorms® EV3 application and start a new program named Robot Arm. Make sure that the large motors are connected through the B and C ports in the bottom right-hand corner of the application and your medium motor is shown in port A in the bottom right-hand corner of the application.

On the bottom of the screen, open the green tab to use action blocks. Drag the Medium motor block into the workspace and attach it to the Start block. The Medium motor block can be modified in largely the same ways as the Large motor blocks. The mode of the block can be changed to On for seconds, degrees, or rotations, and the speed and unit values

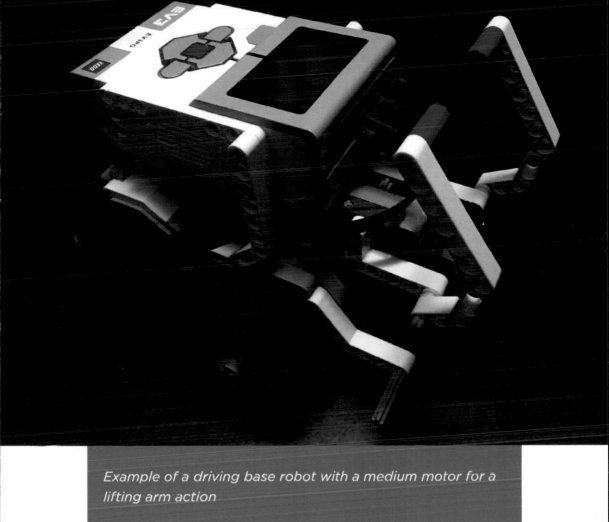

Example of a driving base robot with a medium motor for a lifting arm action

can be altered as well. The most important thing to remember when using the medium motor for the lifting arm is that the degrees of rotation are limited by the position of the arm. Therefore, it is necessary to monitor the location and position of the arm to make sure the programming instructions do not force it to hyperextend. If the arm is told to move in a direction it should not, the robot's pieces could be bent or broken.

On for degrees is the best option mode in this particular robot build for the Medium motor. It is possible to use positive or negative values for degrees or speed, which controls the direction the motor will move. Pay close attention to the starting place of the degrees of the motor by looking in the bottom right-hand corner to see Medium motor—it will display the current degree value there.

Start with a small number of degrees—below ninety—in the Medium motor block to move the arm until it is possible to determine the exact number of degrees that will be needed for the program. Be sure to reset the arm between each execution of the program as well. For the first run of the program, set the arm to be as high as it can go. With the first Medium motor block, lower the arm over the top of an object sitting directly in front of the robot. This object can be anything small and light. Set the speed at 30 and the degree value at –90.

Test this first part of the program to see if it will lower the arm by the correct number of degrees. Adjust as needed—depending on the object that the arm is trying to move, it may be necessary to increase the degrees as much as –120. Then, add a Move Steering block after the Medium motor block and set it to move backward by using a negative value for the speed. Add one more Medium motor block after that to move the arm upward, releasing the object the robot is supposed to move. For this block, use the same degree value as before, but this time, it should be a positive value so that the motor will move in the opposite direction. Thus, it will lift the arm rather than lower it. With all this in place, click Start to execute the program. Did the robot move as expected, and did it move the object well? What could be done to improve the program?

Try modifying your program so that the robot uses its arm to push an object instead of pulling it this time. Depending on the size of the object, it may be necessary to make the arm extremely low so that it pushes the object smoothly instead of just knocking it over. Then, the robot will have to move at an appropriate speed so that it will not get stuck behind the object, but also will not slip and run the object over. Execute this modified program and see how well it runs this time.

What other uses could you imagine for the robot arm? Consider how the arm could be modified for different uses, such as flipping a switch or scooping up small objects to carry.

Activity 9

Music to My Ears

Robots are typically very good at multitasking— but only if they are programmed effectively. In this activity, the robot will be programmed to multitask by playing a sound and changing its status light at the same time.

For starters, create a new program named Music to My Ears in the the LEGO Mindstorms® EV3 application. This program will use the multitasking feature that allows the robot to read and execute more than one string of code simultaneously.

Open the green tab at the bottom of the screen to use the action blocks. Drag the Sound block into the workspace and attach it to the Start block. Change the mode of the Sound block to play a tone; choose any sound by clicking on the parameter under Hz and selecting a note. After this, select the value for the duration of the note. Then, drag a Brick status light block into the workspace.

Multitasking will be used to drag a connector from the Start block to the Sound block and the Brick status light block so that both of these action blocks will occur simultaneously. Click on the orange tab to view the necessary control flow blocks. Add a Wait block at the end of each of the Sound and Brick status light blocks.

Click the Start button to execute the program and determine its success. Did the lights and sound do what was expected? Try modifying the program so that the lights flash between two colors and the sound block plays two different notes. To do this, add another Sound block after the Wait block and select a different note. Then, add another Brick display lights block to the end of the Wait block on the other string and select a different color. Do not forget to add a Wait block to the end of each string of code. The end result of these modifications should look like a path split into two branches; each should have four blocks.

What might this program look like if a Loop block was added around each string of code? How could the loop be used to control the number of times the lights flashed or the robot played those notes? This would make the program a more advanced form of multitasking.

Activity 10

Simon Says

This activity will make use of both the color sensor and the multitasking skills of previous activities to program the robot to execute a different action for each of four colors it might detect. Think of it like a game of Simon Says—for robots. When the color sensor (Simon) sees a specific color, it tells the robot to do a specific task. For example, when red is detected, move forward; when yellow is detected, move backward. This is where multitasking comes in: the color sensor needs to constantly search for each of four colors and then execute the correct line of code depending on which color it senses.

For this activity, make sure the color sensor is installed on the robot; it should be facing forward. Then, open up the LEGO Mindstorms® EV3 application, start a new program, and name it Simon Says. Make sure that the large motors are connected through the B and C ports in the bottom right-hand corner of the application; take note of the angle value for both motors. In the same location, the color sensor should also display as being detected in port three.

Open up the orange tab in the application to use the control flow blocks. Drag the Loop block into the workspace and attach it to the Start block. This loop will need to use multitasking so the robot can continuously search for certain colors and then execute its programming command when they are detected. Therefore, the Loop block should remain in an unlimited loop. For each of four main colors—red, blue, green, yellow, for example—drag a Wait block inside the Loop block. Connect the loop to each of the four Wait blocks with multitasking wires linking each one. Change the mode of each Wait block to Color Sensor—Compare—Color, then select one of the four colors for each Wait block. After the Wait block, determine what the robot should be doing upon seeing that color. For example, maybe the robot should move, make a sound, or display an image when a certain color is seen. Make sure the commands are different for each color, so it will be easy to tell which color the sensor is detecting.

Click the Start button to execute the program. Was the robot able to successfully detect the correct color? Did any of the action blocks tied to a specific color not function properly? It is possible that it may be necessary to add an additional Wait block after

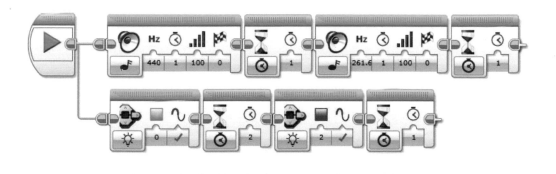

Give this modified program a try to see how it runs.

each action and set it for a short time to give the robot a pause between searching for colors.

After learning more about using control flow blocks and the color sensor, think about other ways to create a similar program. What applications could this type of program have in the real world—why would a robot need to identify colors and react in a different way depending on the color observed?

Activity 11

Stay in Shape

Telling a robot to move forward is relatively easy, but working in turns can be a little trickier. Using a gyro sensor to program more precise turns is one obvious answer to keeping things sharp. The LEGO Mindstorms® EV3 gyro sensor can be programmed to turn for an exact number of degrees. Add in a loop to program a perfect square and triangle. How does this compare with simply using the tank block and adjusting the parameters and values to create each angle? For one thing, it will be much cleaner and easier to calculate.

For this activity, it will be necessary to add the gyro sensor to the top of the robot. The gyro sensor can measure rotational motion as well as the rate of rotation. It can be programmed to detect how far a robot has turned or to make something else happen at a certain point in a rotation. All of these functions will be important.

With the gyro sensor installed, create a new program named Stay in Shape in the LEGO Mindstorms® EV3 application. Make sure that the large motors are connected through the B and C ports in the bottom right-hand corner of the application. In the same location, the gyro sensor should also display as being detected in port two.

In the application, start off by going into the green action block tab. Drag the Move Tank block into the workspace and attach it to the Start block. The robot should start this program by turning until it has turned a certain number of degrees. To accomplish this, set the mode for the Move Tank block to On and set the parameters so that one motor is set to a speed of 0 and the other somewhere from 30 to 50. Click on the orange tab to view control flow blocks and drag a Wait block into the workspace; attach it to the Move Tank block. Change the mode of the Wait block to Gyro sensor—Change—Angle. Change the parameters to Increase, by 90. Then switch back to the action blocks tab and drag another Move Tank block to the end of the Wait block. Set this Move Tank block to On for rotations; decrease the speed in both motors, but keep them equal and set the value for number of rotations to either 1 or 2.

Click the Start button to execute the program. The robot should have turned—did it? Would any adjustments be needed to make a more accurate right-angle turn?

Try modifying the program by putting all these blocks inside of a Loop block; setting the mode to Count; and changing the value to match the number of turns needed to make the robot create a shape, like a square. Consider what degree of a turn would be required for the shape you would like to replicate and how many sides that shape has. Adjust the program to reflect the number of degrees needed for each turn and the number of turns that would need to be made within the Loop block to create the shape.

   With this in mind, think about how the gyro sensor helps with creating a shape. Does using a sensor to detect degrees change the number of times needed to test the program to make sure a turn is accurate?

Career Connections

Despite being a relatively futuristic topic, the word "robot" entered the English language all the way back in 1920 after it appeared in a play—*R.U.R.: Rossum's Universal Robots*—written by Karel Čapek. Though this drama was intended to be a warning about the dangers of an automated machine, technology has changed, evolved, and advanced to the point that robotics is a field at the very forefront of exciting technical innovations in the twenty-first century.

Companies of all shapes and sizes, the most famous being Boston Dynamics, are invested heavily in greater innovation and more widespread use of robots. Some industries, such as automobile manufacturing, use robotic implements on a daily basis to improve productivity and safety in the workplace. Robots are good at many things humans are not—one of the most obvious being incredible precision. In some cutting-edge hospitals, surgeons use robotic arms to assist in delicate procedures in which attention to detail is absolutely crucial. Behind every robot in every industry is a coder—or team of coders—who made it possible for this amazing technology to be used by a regular person.

Without the code that makes a robot run, it is nothing but a pretty machine. For that reason, there

Robotics are being used more and more in advanced manufacturing as a way of boosting efficiency and productivity while being cost effective in the long term.

are countless jobs in the field of robotics available to programmers who know how to make machines move. Studying computer science is the first step in a long journey of technology-based discovery that can lead to highly desirable careers in the tech industry. On top of that, as robots continue to take over such diverse fields as agriculture, medicine, manufacturing, and more, demand for skilled programmers and robot enthusiasts will only continue to go up across the

More schools are introducing robots and programming instruction to prepare students for possible future education and careers in these growing fields.

board. This is good news for students and admirers of computer science.

The explosive job market in programming fields in the twenty-first century—especially in the 2010s and onward into the 2020s—has made learning more about computers and how they work more important than ever before. Learning how to code has its own benefits, such as career preparedness in software development fields, and it is directly related to a strong foundational understanding of robotics. Many public schools now include a basic background of computer science in their curriculum, and robots are increasingly a part of that study. This is because there are clear benefits to learning about the intersection of robotics and coding, not the least of which being the rapidly evolving job market.

Though economic pressures, innovations, and demands change the job market on a daily basis, there is one sector that is always on the rise: technology. There are breakthroughs happening each and every day in dozens of computer science–related fields, and someone with a strong knowledge of programming will have greater access to countless jobs that are continuously created by technology companies, big and small. Advanced robotics and computer science knowledge is even being applied to some industries that many analysts believed were dead or dying, such as manufacturing in the United States. Though this industry has been declining in both profitability and popularity in the United States—with millions of jobs outsourced to other countries—for decades, the introduction of robots and other tech innovations in the late 2010s have led to a comeback in American jobs in manufacturing. These jobs require highly skilled candidates, and many come along with a healthy salary, to boot.

Learning how to program with robots of any kind will bring anyone closer to preparing for a career in a multitude of fields. In addition to manufacturing,

Robotic arms are being used in a variety of fields to do jobs more efficiently and consistently than human hands. They offer many advantages to businesses.

the industries of transportation, health care, and agriculture are increasingly utilizing robots and automation to increase efficiency, productivity, or to go where humans cannot go. Even if these are not the fields in which you have a passion, learning computer programming can open doors to a multitude of different career paths, including computer programmer, software developer, information technology consultant, web developer, health information technician, video game designer, mobile application developer, user interface designer, and more. Above all, leaders recruiting the future

Transportation and logistics, technology, and automotive companies have taken the lead in utilizing robotics in advanced manufacturing.

workforce are going to be looking for candidates that are comfortable with changing technology, creativity, and innovation. Having a foundation of knowledge in computer science—and especially a familiarity with robots—will make your natural talent shine through, increasing your chances of landing a high-profile job in the industry of your choice.

Glossary

application A type of computer software that performs a specific function for the user.

attachment A device, tool, or extension that can be added onto the base of a robot.

automated Able to complete a task without human supervision or input.

Bluetooth A wireless technology that allows communication between enabled devices.

brick The control center and power source for a LEGO Mindstorms® EV3 robot.

conditional statement A statement describing a set of instructions performed when certain conditions are met.

curriculum The courses and standards offered or followed by a school.

default The basic rules or instructions to be followed if no parameters are specified.

device A unit of hardware, outside or inside, a housing case.

execute Of a program or robot: to complete the steps of a computer program.

explosive Describing something that is experiencing very fast growth.

flow control Parts of code that regulate or alter the transmission of data or instructions in a program.

gyro Short for "gyroscopic," describing something that measures angular or rotational speed and orientation.

hyperextended Moved dangerously beyond normal limitations; can result in harm or damage.

if-then In computer science: a statement that instructs a program to check a condition.

innovations Advances or breakthroughs, particularly relevant to technological progress.

intersection A point or area at which two or more different things meet.

intuitive Easy to use or understand.

loop A sequence of directions that is repeated until a certain condition is met.

manufacturing An industry in which goods are produced.

mode A distinct setting with a computer program or specific block of code.

modify To change or alter, typically to improve the result of a program.

multitasking A process that allows for more than one computer task to be performed at a time.

navigate To successfully find a way through something.

outsourced Describing jobs that—formerly done domestically—are now done abroad.

parameter A kind of variable in a computer program that sets a definition for or boundaries to something.

precise Extremely accurate or delicate.

robust Having a full feature set and many options.

sensor A device that detects and responds to a certain type of input from the physical environment.

threshold A predetermined boundary or limit at or after which something happens.

ultrasonic Describing something having a frequency above human hearing.

value The representation of some data that can be manipulated in a computer program.

variable A type of data in computer science that is not fixed, or can be changed.

workspace The blank space designated for moving together blocks of code to create a program.

For More Information

Code.org
1501 4th Avenue, Suite 900
Seattle, WA 98101
Website: https://code.org/learn/robotics
Facebook: @Code.org
Instagram and Twitter: @codeorg
Code.org's mission is to expand access to computer science in schools; it organizes an annual Hour of Code event to further this mission. Its free website contains games and activities that teach concepts of computer science and coding, as well as activities for a variety of different robotics systems.

FIRST Robotics Canada
PO Box 518, Pickering Main
Pickering, ON L1V 2R7
Canada
Website: https://www.firstroboticscanada.org
Facebook and Instagram: @FIRSTRoboticsCanada
Twitter: @CANFIRST
The FIRST LEGO League in Canada is an organization that organizes an annual EV3 robotics challenge based on a real-world problem. It also generally helps Canadian students break into the fields of computer science and robotics.

iD Tech
910 East Hamilton Avenue, Suite 300
Campbell, CA 95008
(888) 709-8324
Website: https://www.idtech.com
Facebook: @computercamps
Instagram: @idtech
Twitter: @iDTechCamps
iD Tech is one of the leading organizations for
    computer science–based summer camp offerings
    in the United States and around the world. It
    offers coding camps with a goal to increase
    participation for girls, prepare kids for a future
    in STEM careers, and provide scholarships for
    underserved populations.

Institute of Robotics & Intelligent Systems (IRIS)
1111 Albion Road, Unit G1
Etobicoke, ON M9V 1A9
Canada
(416) 619-5229
Website: https://iriscanada.com
Facebook and Twitter: @intelligentrobo
Also known as IRIS, this organization is committed
    to bringing robotics education to everyone
    and promoting the study of robots. It offers a
    wide variety of programming camps at multiple
    locations throughout Canada.

LEGO Education
501 Boylston Street, Suite 4103
Boston, MA 02116
(800) 362-4308
Website: https://education.lego.com/en-us
Facebook: @LEGOEducationOfficial
Instagram: @legoeducation
Twitter: @LEGO_Education
This site offers visitors the chance to purchase kits
   as well as featuring a number of great resources,
   including quick-start guides, troubleshooting tips,
   and lesson plans.

National Robotics Engineering Center (NREC)
10 40th Street
Pittsburgh, PA 15201
(412) 681-6900
Website: https://www.nrec.ri.cmu.edu
Facebook: @NationalRobotics
Twitter: @nrec_cmu
Sponsored by Carnegie Mellon University, NREC is
   responsible for advancing robotics education
   and initiatives all around the United States. Its
   website features news and other information about
   the field.

For Further Reading

Baum, Margaux, and Simone Payment. *Building a Career in Robotics*. New York, NY: The Rosen Publishing Group, 2018.

Baum, Margaux, and Joel Chaffee. *Engineering and Building Robots for Competitions*. New York, NY: Rosen Publishing, 2018.

Baum, Margaux, and Jeri Freedman. *The History of Robots and Robotics*. New York, NY: Rosen Publishing, 2018.

Hardyman, Robyn. *Robotics in Medicine*. New York, NY: Greenhaven Publishing, 2018.

Isogawa, Yoshihito. *The LEGO Mindstorms EV3 Idea Book: 181 Simple Machines and Clever Contraptions*. San Francisco, CA: No Starch Press, 2015.

La Bella, Laura. *The Future of Robotics*. New York, NY: Rosen Publishing, 2018.

Martin, Claudia. *Robotics in Law Enforcement*. New York, NY: Greenhaven Publishing, 2018.

Martin, Claudia. *Robotics in Industry*. New York, NY: Greenhaven Publishing, 2018.

Rusch, Elizabeth. *Mighty Mars Rovers: The Incredible Adventures of Spirit and Opportunity*. Boston, MA: HMH Books for Young Readers, 2017.

Snedden, Robert. *Robotics in Space*. New York, NY: Greenhaven Publishing, 2018.

Bibliography

Brubaker, Olivia. "Robots Are Changing The World." EdX Blog, April 6, 2017. https://blog.edx.org/robots-changing-world.

Flatow, Ira. "Science Diction: The Origin of the Word 'Robot'." NPR, April 22, 2011. https://www.npr.org/2011/04/22/135634400/science-diction-the-origin-of-the-word-robot.

Harris, Patricia. *Understanding Coding with LEGO Mindstorms*. New York, NY: PowerKids Press, 2016.

Lego Education. "LEGO Mindstorms EV3 User Guide." Retrieved April 19, 2019. https://le-www-live-s.legocdn.com/ev3/userguide/1.4.0/ev3_userguide_enus.pdf.

Lynch, Matthew. "Five Reasons to Teach Robotics in Schools." The Tech Edvocate, March 26, 2017. http://www.thetechedvocate.org/five-reasons-to-teach-robotics-in-schools.

Sykes, Nathan. "How Manufacturing Automation Is Evolving." Robotics Business Review, March 7, 2018. https://www.roboticsbusinessreview.com/manufacturing/how-manufacturing-automation-is-evolving.

Index

T

U

V

W

About the Author

Emilee Hillman is a library technologies specialist who spends most of her time training educators and young students in robotics and STEM resources. She has written computational thinking activities for the Rosen Classroom series Computer Science for the Real World as well as the book *Understanding Coding with Java*. Hillman has a master's degree in library science from SUNY Albany and a bachelor's of science in childhood education from The College of Saint Rose. She lives in Rochester, New York, with her husband and two dogs; they are anxiously awaiting the arrival of their first child.

Photo Credits

Cover Bogdan Vija/Shutterstock.com; cover, p. 1 © (code) iStockphoto.com/scanrail; p. 4 Georgijevic/E+/Getty Images; pp. 5, 7, 8 AlesiaKan/Shutterstock.com; p. 9 SpeedKingz/Shutterstock.com; pp. 11, 12, 19, 20, 25, 28, 30, 31, 35, 41 Emilee Hillman ;p. 47 Jensen/Shutterstock.com; p. 48 Monkey Business Images/Shutterstock.com; p. 50 asharkyu/Shutterstock.com; p. 51 Factory_Easy/Shutterstock.com; interior pages border design © iStockphoto.com/Akrain.

Design: Matt Cauli; Editor: Siyavush Saidian; Photo Researcher: Sherri Jackson